MONEY MATTERS

A 31-Day Financial Wellness Journaling Challenge

Indi Writes

Money Matters

Victory Publishing Co
Memphis, TN 38125

Distributed by Indiwrites, www.indiwrites.com

ISBN: 978-1-964284-23-1

Printed in the United States of America

This Journal Belongs to

For the love of money is a root of all kinds of evil. Some people, eager for money, have wandered from the faith and pierced themselves with many griefs.

1 TIMOTHY 6:10

Introduction

Welcome to the "Money Matters" Financial Wellness Challenge, a transformative 31-day journey designed to reshape your relationship with money and foster a deeper understanding of its impact on your life. This challenge is not just about managing finances—it's about achieving holistic well-being through financial wisdom and discipline.

BASIC FINANCIAL SECURITY

This foundational level ensures that your essential needs are met without undue financial strain. It's about stability and the absence of anxiety over financial matters.

FINANCIAL SAFETY

At this level, you have safeguards in place to handle unexpected financial shocks and emergencies. This includes having an emergency fund and insurance protections, providing you with a buffer against life's uncertainties.

FINANCIAL FREEDOM

The ultimate goal of financial well-being, financial freedom, is where you have amassed enough wealth to live comfortably and make life choices that aren't constrained by financial limitations. This level allows you the freedom to pursue your dreams and goals on your own terms.

Starting Your Journey with a Financial Overview

Before diving into the daily prompts, you will begin the challenge by undertaking a financial overview exercise. This includes reviewing your income and spending over the past 30 days and pulling your credit report to check for any inaccuracies. This exercise sets the foundation for a month of learning and growth.:

Review your income and expenses for the previous month. Put all expenses into categories, such as bills, food, entertainment, etc. You can download a budget app such as Rocket Mortgage that connects to your bank account, if your bank does not include expense tracking. Also pull your credit and ensure there are no inaccuracies. Apps such as Credit Karma are free and a great resource.

TOTAL INCOME	TOTAL EXPENSES	TOTAL SAVING

What can you decrease so you can increase in important areas? and how?

TOP 3 SPENDING CATEGORIES

1. ____________________
2. ____________________
3. ____________________

OUTSTANDING DEBT

1. ____________________
2. ____________________
3. ____________________

BUDGET & SAVINGS GOALS

- [ ]
- [ ]
- [ ]
- [ ]
- [ ]
- [ ]
- [ ]

STRATEGY

You are encouraged to select a book on Christian financial stewardship, money mindset, or biblical wealth to accompany this challenge. Space is provided in the back of the journal to take notes, record insights, and track revelations from your reading—creating a complete spiritual and financial wellness experience.

How to take part in this challenge:

- **Read and Write Out the Scripture**: Start by reading the given scripture, ensuring you also read a few passages before and after, or the entire chapter for full understanding.
- **Explore Multiple Translations**: Review the scripture in 1-3 different translations, paying attention to variations in wording.
- **Define Key Verbs**: Look up and write out definitions for key verbs. This practice allows the Holy Spirit to reveal deeper insights.
- **Reflect and Observe:** Write down your observations and any revelations from the text.
- **Answer the Writing Prompt**: Respond to the daily prompt, allowing it to guide your reflections and deepen your understanding.

Participate in the Community:

Share your revelations, responses to the prompts, and engage with others in the Pen Warriors Facebook Community. This collaborative space will enhance your journaling experience, providing support and inspiration from fellow participants. We have bi-monthly live group check in sessions.

Date ____________

01 Assess Your Current Financial Situation

Matthew 6:21

Write out the verse in at least 2-different versions. Then highlight the differences in words used.

What are your initial thoughts? What do you believe God is saying to you?

REFLECT & *React*

Write about your current financial situation. How do you feel about it? What are your financial goals?

Date ____________

02 Reflect on Contentment

1 Timothy 6:6

Write out the verse in at least 2-different versions. Then highlight the differences in words used.

What are your initial thoughts? What do you believe God is saying to you?

REFLECT & *React*

How do you practice contentment in your life? What areas do you struggle with contentment?

Date ____________________

03

God's Provision

Philippians 4:19

Write out the verse in at least 2-different versions. Then highlight the differences in words used.

What are your initial thoughts? What do you believe God is saying to you?

REFLECT & *React*

Write about a time when God provided for your needs in an unexpected way.

Date ____________________

04

Budgeting

Proverbs 21:5

Write out the verse in at least 2-different versions. Then highlight the differences in words used.

What are your initial thoughts? What do you believe God is saying to you?

REFLECT & *React*

Reflect on your budgeting habits. How can you improve them to better steward your resources?

Date ____________________

05

The Role of Debt

Proverbs 22:7

Write out the verse in at least 2-different versions. Then highlight the differences in words used.

What are your initial thoughts? What do you believe God is saying to you?

REFLECT & *React*

What are your thoughts on debt? How has debt affected your life?

Date ____________

06

Generosity

2 Corinthians 9:7

Write out the verse in at least 2-different versions. Then highlight the differences in words used.

What are your initial thoughts? What do you believe God is saying to you?

REFLECT & *React*

How do you practice generosity? Write about a time you felt blessed through giving.

Date ____________

07 Savings and Investments

Proverbs 21:20

Write out the verse in at least 2-different versions. Then highlight the differences in words used.

What are your initial thoughts? What do you believe God is saying to you?

REFLECT & *React*

Reflect on your saving habits. Are you preparing for future needs and opportunities?

"If we command our wealth, we shall be rich and free. If our wealth commands us, we are poor indeed."

– Edmund Burke

Date

08 Trusting God with Finances

Proverbs 3:5

Write out the verse in at least 2-different versions. Then highlight the differences in words used.

What are your initial thoughts? What do you believe God is saying to you?

REFLECT & *React*

How do you practice trusting God with your financial concerns and decisions?

Date ____________________

09

Financial Goals

Proverbs 16:3

Write out the verse in at least 2-different versions. Then highlight the differences in words used.

What are your initial thoughts? What do you believe God is saying to you?

REFLECT & *React*

What are your short-term and long-term financial goals? How can you align them with God's will?

Date ____________________

10

Financial Peace

John 14:27

Write out the verse in at least 2-different versions. Then highlight the differences in words used.

What are your initial thoughts? What do you believe God is saying to you?

REFLECT & *React*

Write about what financial peace means to you. How can you achieve it?

Date ____________________

11 Overcoming Financial Fears

2 Timothy 1:7

Write out the verse in at least 2-different versions. Then highlight the differences in words used.

What are your initial thoughts? What do you believe God is saying to you?

REFLECT & React

What financial fears do you have? How can you give them to God?

Date ______________

12

Wisdom in Spending

Hosea 14:9

Write out the verse in at least 2-different versions.Then highlight the differences in words used.

What are your initial thoughts? What do you believe God is saying to you?

REFLECT & *React*

Reflect on your spending habits. How can you spend wisely and honor God with your purchases?

Date ________________

13

Honesty in Finances

Proverbs 28:6

Write out the verse in at least 2-different versions. Then highlight the differences in words used.

What are your initial thoughts? What do you believe God is saying to you?

REFLECT & *React*

How do you practice honesty in your financial dealings? Why is it important?

Date ____________

14

Financial Discipline

Hebrews 12:11

Write out the verse in at least 2-different versions. Then highlight the differences in words used.

What are your initial thoughts? What do you believe God is saying to you?

REFLECT & *React*

Write about a time you exercised financial discipline. How did it benefit you?

"Money is a terrible master but an excellent servant."

– P.T. Barnum

Date ____________

15 Financial Dependence on God

2 Corinthians 9:8

Write out the verse in at least 2-different versions. Then highlight the differences in words used.

What are your initial thoughts? What do you believe God is saying to you?

REFLECT & *React*

How can you practice depending on God for your financial needs?

Date ______________

16

The Purpose of Wealth

Proverbs 3:9

Write out the verse in at least 2-different versions. Then highlight the differences in words used.

What are your initial thoughts? What do you believe God is saying to you?

REFLECT & *React*

Reflect on the purpose of wealth in your life. How can you use it to glorify God?

Date ____________________

17

Financial Temptations

1 Corinthians 10:13

Write out the verse in at least 2-different versions. Then highlight the differences in words used.

What are your initial thoughts? What do you believe God is saying to you?

REFLECT & React

What financial temptations do you face? How can you overcome them with God's help?

Date ____________________

18

Financial Legacy

Proverbs 13:22

Write out the verse in at least 2-different versions. Then highlight the differences in words used.

What are your initial thoughts? What do you believe God is saying to you?

REFLECT & *React*

What kind of financial legacy do you want to leave for your family and others?

Date ____________

19 Seeking Financial Counsel

Proverbs 15:22

Write out the verse in at least 2-different versions. Then highlight the differences in words used.

What are your initial thoughts? What do you believe God is saying to you?

REFLECT & *React*

Write about the importance of seeking wise financial counsel. Who can you turn to for advice?

Date ____________________

20

Financial Blessings

1 Chronicles 16:34

Write out the verse in at least 2-different versions. Then highlight the differences in words used.

What are your initial thoughts? What do you believe God is saying to you?

REFLECT & *React*

How have you experienced financial blessings in your life? How can you express gratitude for them?

Date ____________________

21

Avoiding Greed

Luke 12:15

Write out the verse in at least 2-different versions.Then highlight the differences in words used.

What are your initial thoughts? What do you believe God is saying to you?

REFLECT & *React*

How do you guard against greed in your financial decisions?

"Financial peace isn't the acquisition of stuff. It's learning to live on less than you make, so you can give money back and have money to invest. You can't win until you do this."

– Dave Ramsey

Date ______________

22

Financial Stewardship

1 Corinthians 4:2

Write out the verse in at least 2-different versions. Then highlight the differences in words used.

What are your initial thoughts? What do you believe God is saying to you?

REFLECT & *React*

Reflect on how you can be a better steward of the resources God has given you

Date ____________

23 Balancing Needs and Wants

Hebrews 13:5

Write out the verse in at least 2-different versions. Then highlight the differences in words used.

What are your initial thoughts? What do you believe God is saying to you?

REFLECT & *React*

How do you differentiate between needs and wants in your spending?

Date

24

Financial Accountability

1 Thessalonians 5:11

Write out the verse in at least 2-different versions. Then highlight the differences in words used.

What are your initial thoughts? What do you believe God is saying to you?

REFLECT & *React*

Who holds you accountable in your financial decisions? How can this help you grow?

Date ______________

25 Impact of Financial Choices

1 Corinthians 10:31

Write out the verse in at least 2-different versions. Then highlight the differences in words used.

What are your initial thoughts? What do you believe God is saying to you?

REFLECT & React

Write about the long-term impact of your financial choices. How can you make decisions that honor God?

Date ____________________

26

Financial Planning

Luke 14:28

Write out the verse in at least 2-different versions. Then highlight the differences in words used.

What are your initial thoughts? What do you believe God is saying to you?

REFLECT & *React*

Reflect on the importance of financial planning. How can you create a plan that aligns with your values and goals?

Date ____________

27

Gratitude for Resources

1 Thessalonians 5:18

Write out the verse in at least 2-different versions. Then highlight the differences in words used.

What are your initial thoughts? What do you believe God is saying to you?

REFLECT & *React*

How can you express gratitude for the resources God has entrusted to you?

Date ____________________

28 Financial Trust in Relationships

Ephesians 4:25

Write out the verse in at least 2-different versions. Then highlight the differences in words used.

What are your initial thoughts? What do you believe God is saying to you?

REFLECT & *React*

Write about how trust plays a role in your financial relationships with family and friends.

"Money does not dictate your lifestyle, It's what you do to get it and how you manage your finances that determines your lifestyle."

– Wayne Chirisa

Date ____________________

29

Financial Sacrifice

Hebrews 13:16

Write out the verse in at least 2-different versions.Then highlight the differences in words used.

What are your initial thoughts? What do you believe God is saying to you?

REFLECT & React

Reflect on a time when you made a financial sacrifice. How did it impact you and others?

Date ____________

30 Seeking God's Guidance

James 1:5

Write out the verse in at least 2-different versions. Then highlight the differences in words used.

What are your initial thoughts? What do you believe God is saying to you?

REFLECT & React

How can you seek God's guidance in your financial decisions? What steps will you take?

Date ____________________

31 Reflection and Commitment

Psalm 37:5

Write out the verse in at least 2-different versions. Then highlight the differences in words used.

What are your initial thoughts? What do you believe God is saying to you?

REFLECT & React

Reflect on what you've learned this month about financial wellness. What commitments will you make moving forward?

Catrin szeme láttára. Egy álom
oztak. Amikor odaért a fürdőszobába,
felnyögött, és saját hangjától megijedve
gés valahonnan mélyről jött, valami olyan
ette. Megnyitotta a hideg vizes csapot, és vizet
anyinger kezdett elmúlni, nem úgy a jelenet em-
z imént a tanúja lett. Még tisztán látta lelki szemei
atrin szemén át látta, és a borzalom szavakkal leírha-
óhte az arcát egy törülközőben, majd letámolygott a konyhá-
pper a tűzhely melletti székén ült, és elmélkedve meredt maga
ét. Andyre pillantott. A lány látta, hogy a macska szeme elkerekedik, a
pupillában hirtelen rettegés jelenik meg. Leugrott a székről, és eltűnt a
maskaajtón keresztül, mielőtt Andy visszahívhatta volna. Csak bámult
utána. Vajon mit látott? Vagy inkább érzékelt valamit? Jobb bele sem
gondolni.
199

Reading Journal

Date started:

Book title: ______

Author: ______

Genre: ______

What I expected from this book:

Why does this book catch my attention?:

Book Notes

Book *Notes*

Book Notes

Book Notes

Book Notes

Book Notes

Book Notes

Book *Notes*

Book Notes

Book Notes

thank you

Now that you have completed this journal. Go back and read over it to see your growth and progress. You may click the QR code below to use our GROWTH check questionnaire which will be submitted to our admin team and receive a response via email plus access to a discounted follow-up session.

Prompted Journals

1.

EMBRACE YOUR HEALING

Not sure where to start your healing process, this journal will help you face the woman in the mirror, invite God into your broken places and seek the bible for solutions.

2.

ARISE & BUILD

Not satisfied at your current job but know God called you to build a business. This journal will help you tackle your fears while building your business.

3.

BE LOVED

Past failures in love and relationships can make you forget who you are in Christ. This journal will help you develop that transparent relationship with God and restore your rightful place in Him as His daughter.

4.

THRIVE

Created for the women who has suffered Domestic Violence or Sexual Abuse to help her release the blame, learn to forgive, share her testimony and uncover purpose in her pain.

Plus many more

www.indiwrites.com

Who Are We?

IndiWrites is a spiritual growth and development company dedicated to the emotional well-being and christian growth of women in every area of their lives. As a survivor of great trauma, when I finally decided to be consistent in my walk with the Lord, I found that there was residue from my past that greatly influenced my behaviors and thought processes. These behaviors and thoughts hindered how I saw God, myself and others, as well as caused great warfare in the pursuit of my relationships and dreams. Healing is a continuous journey but I'm a firm believer that wholeness is the key to unlocking the abundant life Christ promised us in His word. Our books and journals promise to provide you not just quotes and scriptures but a guide to live this life with faith, confidence, purpose, fearlessness, and tenacity.

Thank you!

For entrusting your journey with us!
Be sure to leave us a review.

Indiana Tuggle